Contemporary Modal Pieces

by Margaret Brandman

Exclusive Distributors for Australia and New Zealand
Encore Music Distributors 227 Napier St. Fitzroy. 3065 Victoria Australia
Ph +61 3 9415 6677 Facsimile 61 3 9415 6655
Email sales@encoremusic.com.au

This book © Copyright 2021 by Margaret Brandman trading as Jazzem Music
46 Gerrale St, Cronulla NSW 2230 Australia

ISBN 978-0-949683-24-3
ORDER NUMBER MMP 8021

International Copyright Secured (APRA/AMCOS) All Rights Reserved
www.margaretbrandman.com

Unauthorised reproduction of any part of this publication by any means including photocopying is an infringement of copyright.

Illustrations by Désirée Van Loan

INTRODUCTION

The *Contemporary Piano Method* is designed to equip the student with the necessary skills to play both Classical and Modern (Popular and Jazz) music, with ease and understanding while giving experience in skills required for both classical and contemporary examination syllabi. The piano method is the central core of an integrated course which provides materials for ear-training (audio and workbooks), theory, improvisation, technique and repertoire pieces in all styles.

Contemporary Modal Pieces provides additional repertoire to complement Books 2A through to Book 4 of the Contemporary Piano Method. Several of the pieces, can be heard on on the CD 'IMAGES' (Order Number MMP 8015)

The pieces in this book explore several contemporary writing techniques in a tuneful and accessible way. They serve to familiarise the performer with tonalities other than Major and Minor. Modal, Pentatonic and Whole-tone scale sounds are explored, as well as the pieces written with serial techniques. The student of serious music will be opened up to the world of Jazz sounds via the Modal scales and the various rhythms explored throughout the book. In addition to the pieces there are many helpful suggestions which provide a means of encouraging improvisation. For the student of composition, previously dry theoretical concepts come alive in the context of the pieces, bridging the gap between conventional writing techniques on the one hand and contemporary experimental material and Jazz compositions on the other.

Before beginning to play these pieces students should have a knowledge of the keyboard geography of major, minor and modal scales. Refer to the supporting publication *Pictorial Patterns for Keyboard Scales and Chords* for graphics of these patterns.

For further explanation on the topic of Modes, students are advised to refer to:
  1) Contemporary Piano Method : Books 3 & 4
  2) Contemporary Theory Workbook: Book 2
  3) Contemporary Chord Workbooks 1 & 2

To familiarise themselves with the sounds of the modes students refer to Contemporary Aural Course: Set 7 (Hear Your Chords!) & Set 8 (Hear More Chords!)

For more detailed information on the ideas and information in the series refer to my web site.

www.margaretbrandman.com

Margaret Brandman
B.Mus.(Comp), T.Mus.A
F.Comp. (ASMC)., F.Mus.Ed.ASMC., L.Perf. (ASMC)
Hon.FNMSM., A.Mus.A., ASA T.Dip.

CONTENTS

	Page
On Modal music	5
Table of Modes	6
Modal Sounds and a list of other scales used in this book	7
Seventh Chords built on the Modes	8
All the Modes transposed to C and the relevant chords	9

	TITLE	MODE	TIME-SIGN	STYLE	
No 1	The Albino Koala	Dorian		Canon. No bar lines	10-11
No 2	The Koala – a tree dweller	Pentatonic	3/4	Changing Registers	12-13
No 3	The Swamp Rat	Dorian	4/4	Syncopation, changing Registers	14-15
No 4	The Noisy Bush, 1 and 2	Pentatonic	(1) 4/4	Clusters	
			(2) Free	Ripples	16-17
No 5	The Pretty-faced Wallaby	Æolian	4/4	Syncopation	18-20
No 6	The Tasmanian Devil	Serial		Irregular Bar lines	21
No 7	Bell-birds	Phrygian	5/4 – 3/4	Chords, Two-octave Unison	22-23
No 8	Kangaroos at the Water-hole	Lydian	3/4 – 6/4	4th chords (Quartal Harmony)	24-25
No 9	The Ring-tail 'Possum	Dorian	Changing	Three-octave Unisons	26-27
No 10	Riverside Scene	Lydian	Irregular	Chords	28-29
No 11	The Rare New-Holland Mouse	Whole-tone	4/4	16ths. Staccato	30-31
No 12	The Wombat	Phrygian	3/4	Canon. Registers	32-33
No 13	The Squirrel-glider	Dorian	7/8	4ths and 5ths	34-35
No 14	The Spiny Ant-eater	Serial	Free	Clusters	36-37
No 15	The Mountain Pygmy 'Possum	Æolian	4/4	Broken chords, 16ths	38-39
No 16	The Short-nosed Bandicoot	Mixolydian	5/4	Canon	40-41
No 17	The Grey Kangaroo	Phrygian	3/4	Syncopation	42-43
No 18	The Great Glider 'Possum	Phrygian	Free	Chords	44-45
No 19	The Red Kangaroo	Lydian	7/8	3rds and 5ths	46-47
No 20	The Emu	Locrian	4/4	Chords	48-49
No 21	The Platypus	Pentatonic	4/4	Black notes only	50-51
Appendix			A Guide to Chord Symbols		52

THE MODES

The Modes were the basis of most music written before the advent of tempered tuning and the major-minor system. From the earliest known church music and folk music through to the music of Palestrina and Byrd in the sixteenth century, modal scales were the basis of composition. There are even traces of Modal influences in the music of the Baroque composers, Bach and Handel, and they occur as scalic sections in the music of Mozart and Beethoven.

With tempered tuning came an increased use of chromaticism and the gradual loss of modal sounds. It was not until the chromatic system had been fully explored at the end of the nineteenth century that composers began to look back to the Modes as an alternative method of composition. Debussy in particular not only used Modal sounds but also the Pentatonic and Whole-tone scales sounds demonstrated in this book.

From the Twentieth Century onward music in the New Age, Ambient and Contemporary genres along with Jazz, Rock and even Heavy Metal styles of music has frequently displayed modal influences.

For a pocket history of the Modes and the development of tempered tuning refer to Book 3 of the *Contemporary Piano Method*.

THE MODES
and how to find them

MODE		FORMULA

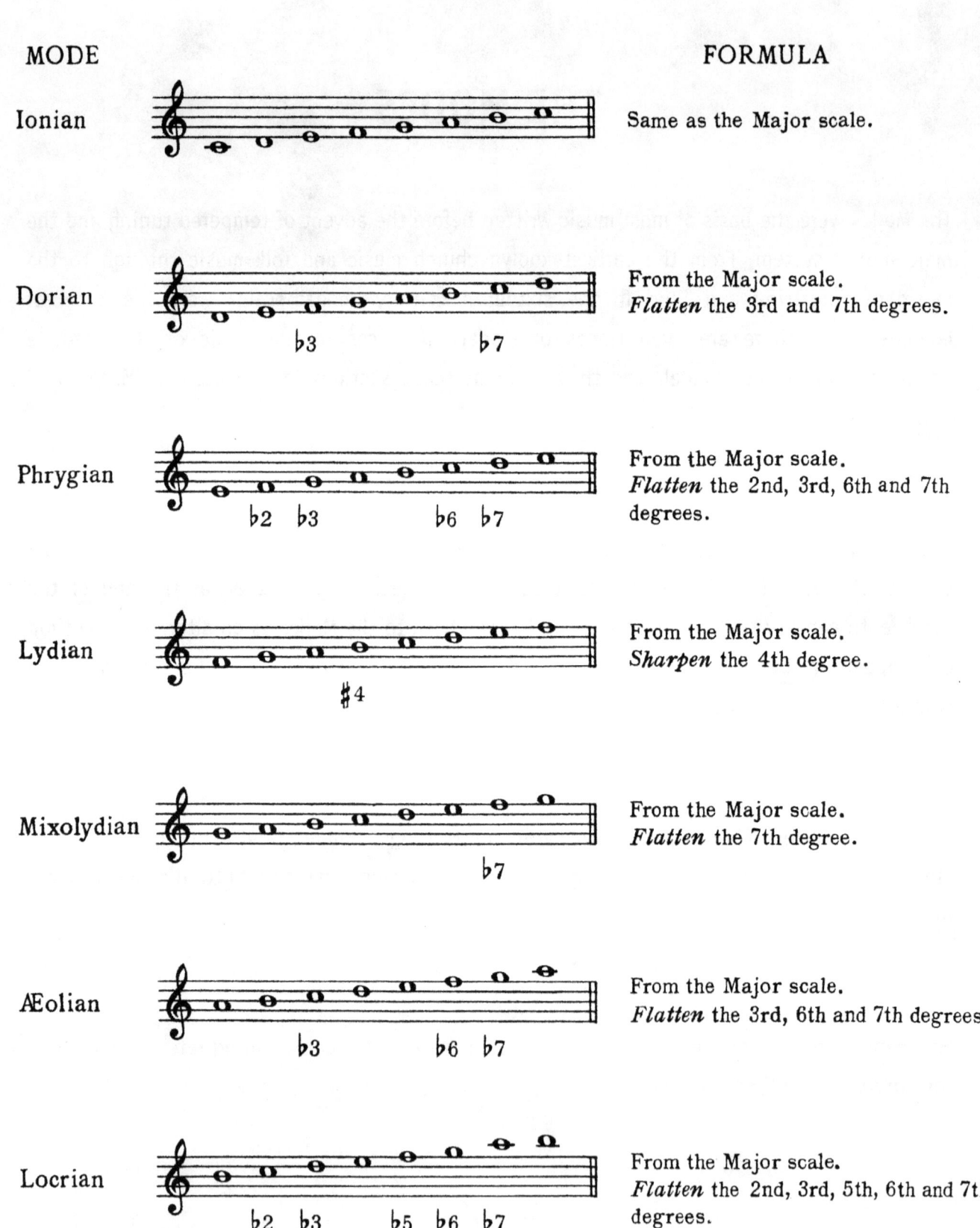

Mode	Formula
Ionian	Same as the Major scale.
Dorian	From the Major scale. *Flatten* the 3rd and 7th degrees.
Phrygian	From the Major scale. *Flatten* the 2nd, 3rd, 6th and 7th degrees.
Lydian	From the Major scale. *Sharpen* the 4th degree.
Mixolydian	From the Major scale. *Flatten* the 7th degree.
Æolian	From the Major scale. *Flatten* the 3rd, 6th and 7th degrees.
Locrian	From the Major scale. *Flatten* the 2nd, 3rd, 5th, 6th and 7th degrees.

Just as the C Major scale pattern (Ionian Mode) can be transposed to all twelve of the notes of the octave, so can the Modes be transposed to any starting note, using the above formulae.

* Refer to Contemporary Theory Workbook - Book 2

MODAL SOUNDS

Positive or Major sounding Modes

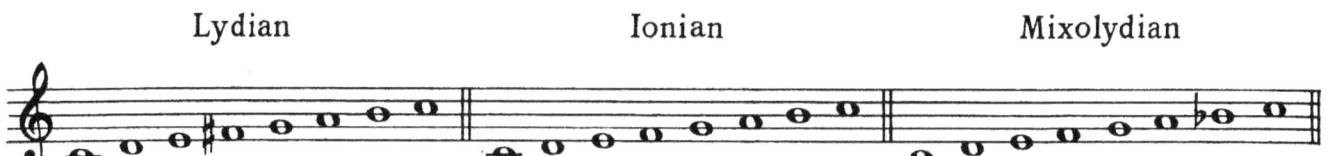

Mode of Median stability

Dorian
(Half-way between Major and minor)

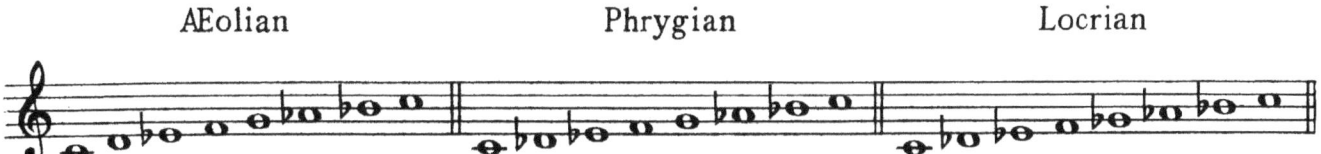

Negative or Minor sounding Modes

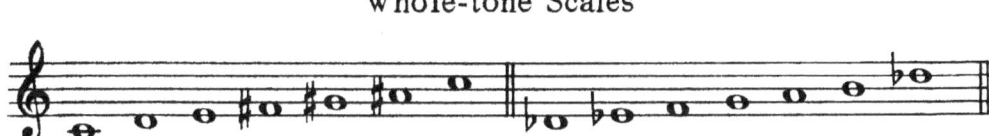

OTHER SCALES USED IN THIS BOOK

Whole-tone Scales

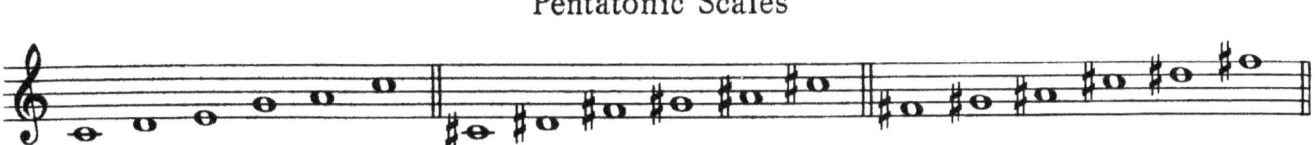

Pentatonic Scales

For further information on these modal other scales, refer to books three and four of the Contemporary Piano Method by the author.

SEVENTH CHORDS BUILT ON THE MODES

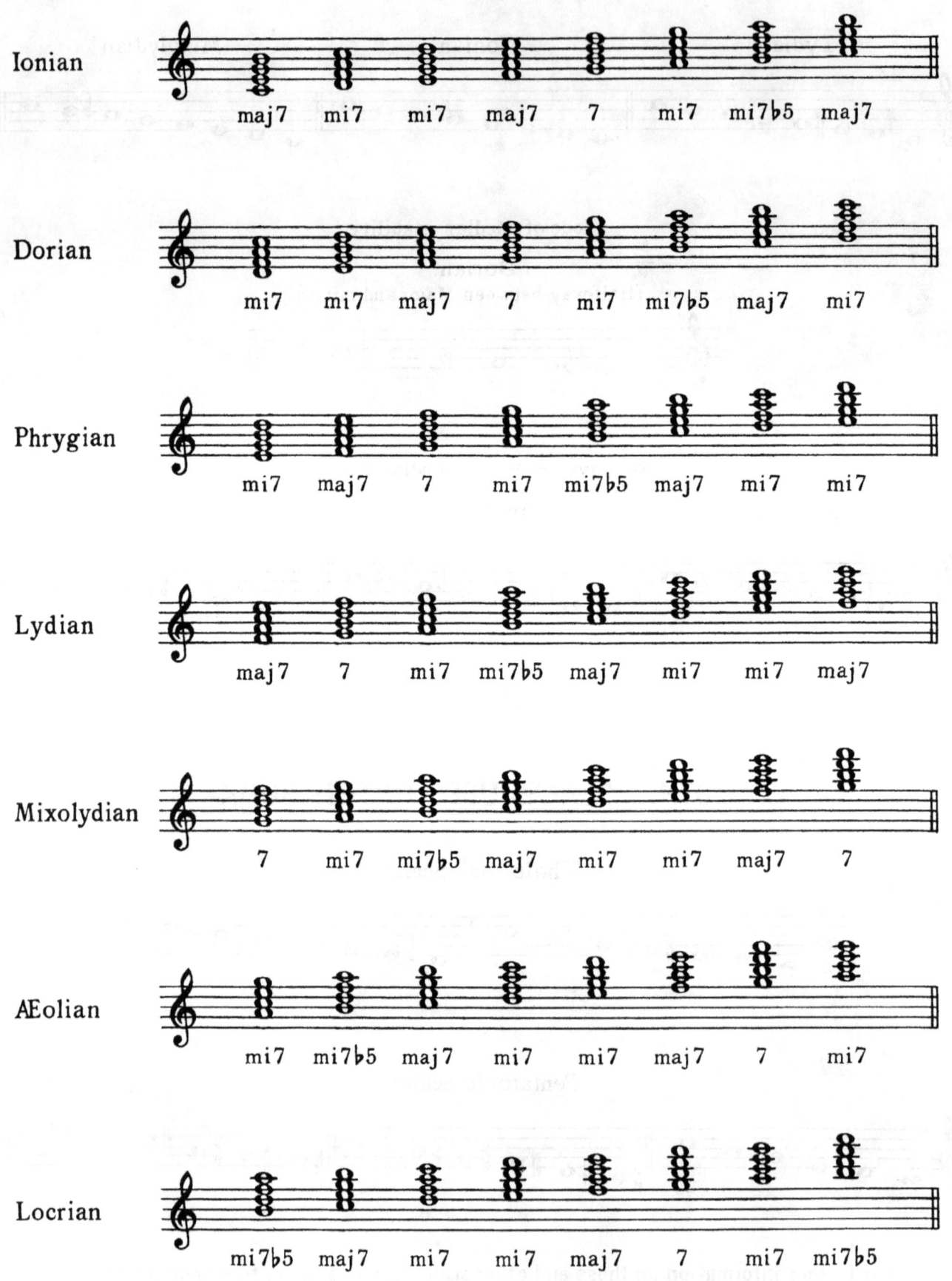

Refer to page 52 for further information on the Chord Symbols, or to the Contemporary Chord Workbook, Book 1, by Margaret Brandman.

USING MODAL SCALES AS IMPROVISATIONAL TOOLS

Below are the transposed forms of all the Modes each using C as the Tonic of the Mode.
The triads, sixths, sevenths and ninths which derive from the Modes are presented alongside.
Each of the Modal scales can be regarded as a suitable scale for improvisation over the derived chords.

For further information on extended chords, that is: elevenths and thirteenths, refer to Book 3 of the Contemporary Piano Method.

THE ALBINO KOALA

CANON

This piece is written as a CANON. A canon is a two-part polyphonic device which is formed when one melody imitates another at a distance. Canons are also known as 'rounds'.

This canon begins with the bass part imitating the treble part at the distance of four quarter-notes and reverses the process in the middle.

To read without bar lines take the quarter note as beat note and make sure you play the notes exactly as spaced on the music.

In this piece, the Dorian Mode is used its in its original form , that is as a white note scale beginning on D.

Note the use of the open hand position over the distance of an octave in the first half of the melody line and the close five-finger hand position in the second half. To learn the piece quickly, block out these two positions.

1. THE ALBINO KOALA

Dorian Mode on D

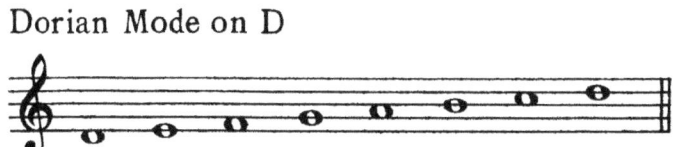

THE KOALA - A TREE DWELLER

This piece suggests the Koala climbing to different parts of the tree. Beginning in the middle, he explores the nether regions and then climbs to the top of the tree where the juiciest leaves are to be found.

Once you have learnt the first eight bars, you will find that the melody line is the same in the next two eight-bar sections. Simply change registers and repeat. When changing positions, try to feel the hand-position movement, allowing each hand to help the other feel the next interval, rather than looking at the hands on the keyboard.

A second person may play this piece as a Canon in a different octave, or on another instrument, beginning either on bar two or three.

IMPROVISATION SUGGESTION

Improvise a Left hand melody line using the Pentatonic scale on 'C', under any or all of the following Right hand chord shapes and clusters, derived from the scale. Aim for 'Eastern. sounds' by using the intervals of fourths and fifths taken from the scale.

2. THE KOALA - A TREE DWELLER

The Swamp Rat

Before playing this piece, play the Mode as a two-octave scale with both hands. Note the pattern of black and white notes on the keyboard, and when playing the piece think of the notes as moving along the pattern.

The left hand notes should be played as block chord shapes before playing as written.

Note that in the second section of the piece, the Right hand part is played an octave higher, (8va). Listen to the varied effect this gives the piece.

Dorian Mode on C

Remember that the pattern of black and white notes on the keyboard for the above mode is the same as the pattern for B flat Major scale.

IMPROVISATION SUGGESTION

Improvise a free piece employing the Dorian Mode on C and any or all of the following chords derived from the scale.

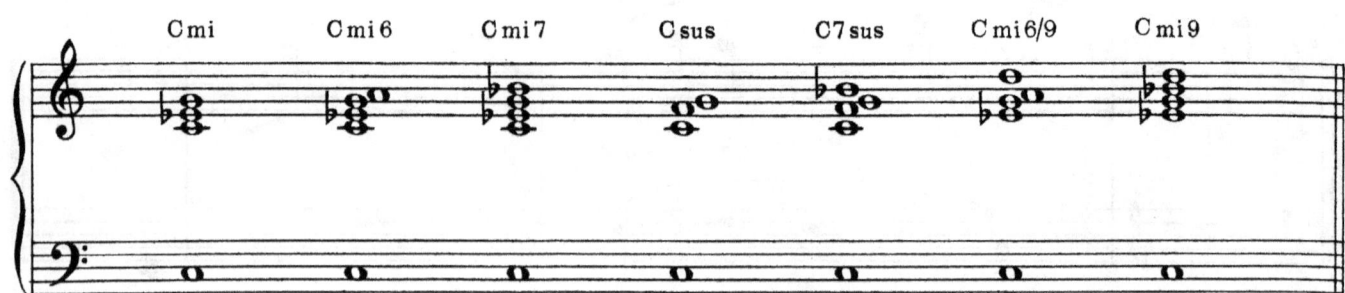

3. THE SWAMP RAT

4. THE NOISY BUSH, 1 AND 2

Pentatonic Scale on C

PART 1. When learning this piece, pick out the very top line, to be played on its own and then do the same with the bottom line. Notice they have the same notes an octave apart. Next play the middle clusters through and then fuse all the parts together.

PART 2. Play the arpeggio then begin on the five-note groups very slowly, picking up speed gradually. The number of repeats suggested is a guide only. The performer may shorten or lengthen each group or add new groups based on the Pentatonic scale given. (See example below.) Keep one group going while the other hand is changing to the next group. The finger action should be light and the pedal changed occasionally. These two pieces may be performed separately or in A B A form.

Pentatonic Scale groups

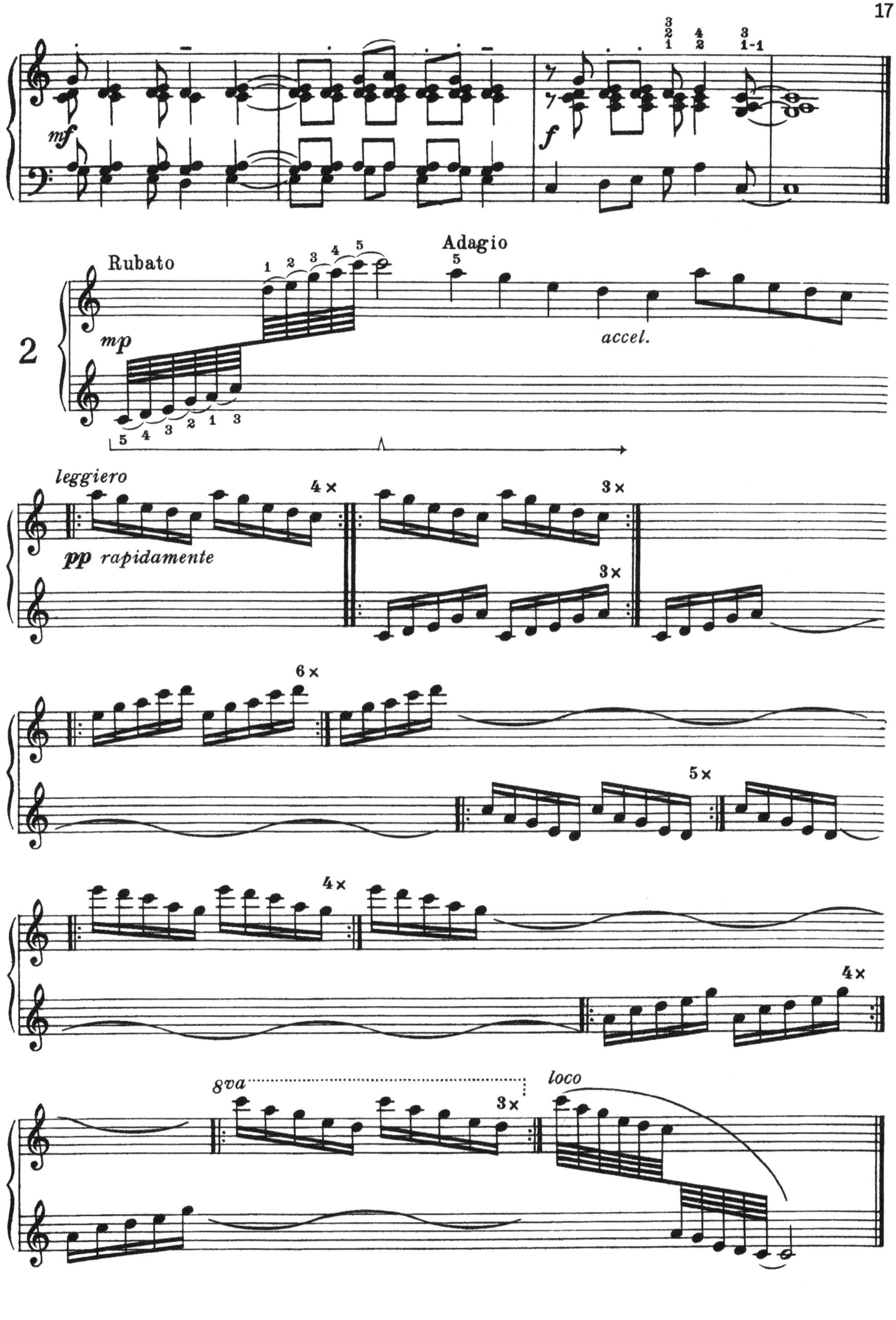
mf
f
2
Rubato
mp
Adagio
accel.
leggiero
pp rapidamente
4×
3×
3×
6×
5×
4×
4×
8va
3×
loco

5. THE PRETTY FACED WALLABY

Æolian Mode on A

Exercise:
Complete the seventh chords above each scale note then name and play each one.

This piece is an excellent vehicle for the study of syncpoation. It sounds equally well at either a moderate or fast speed. Try to achieve a contrast between the hopping effect of the first section and the gliding effects in the middle section.

6. THE TASMANIAN DEVIL
A Serial Composition

THE ROW

This piece is constructed according to the rules of serial composition, which Arnold Schonberg, 1874-1951, devised in the early Twentieth century.

The twelve notes of the chromatic scale are taken at random and then placed in a 'row', which can be used forwards, backwards, inverted or inverted backwards. Most pieces written serially display wide use of angular intervals and try to avoid ordinary chord sequences. *

For more information on Serial Music refer to the Contemporary Piano Method, Book 4, by Margaret Brandman

BELL-BIRDS

Phrygian Mode on E

Play the chord analysis below prior to starting this piece.

When approaching the music, play the first chord in each bar, then move both hands on the second beat of the bar, and then, having played beats three and four, move the hands back on beat five to the position for the chord.

Hint: The notes on the leger lines are in fact exactly two octaves from the left hand notes. Pedal carefully to sustain the sounds while the hands are moving.

THE HARMONIC SCHEME

Chord analysis

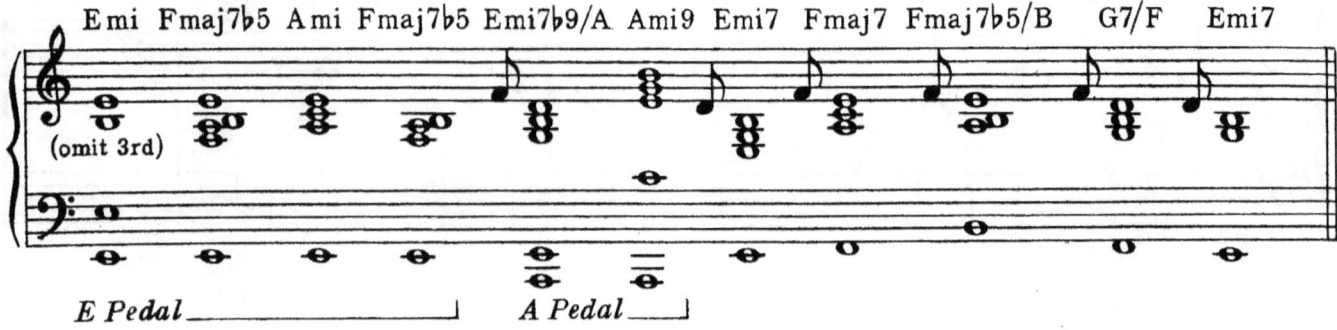

* See page 52 for Chord Symbols

7. BELLBIRDS

KANGAROOS AT THE WATER-HOLE

Lydian Mode on F

Types of chords found in the Lydian Mode

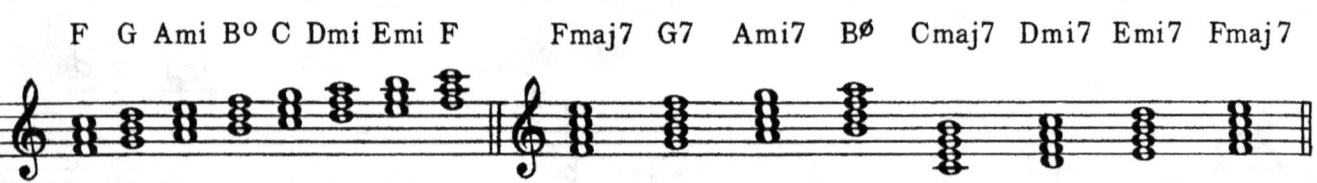

See page 52 for Chord Symbols

Chord Analysis

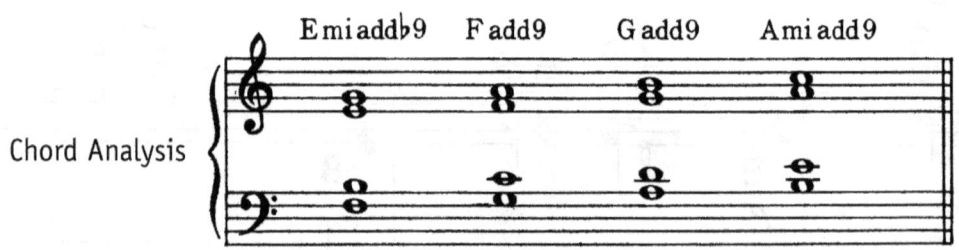

8. KANGAROOS AT THE WATER-HOLE

Take this piece slowly and watch the staccato chords and fingering carefully.

Improvisation suggestion

Improvise a short piece based on the Lydian Mode on F as a basis for your melody.
Use any or all of the chords listed on the facing page as a basis for the harmony.

THE RING-TAIL 'POSSUM

Dorian Mode on G

Remember that this Mode has the same pattern of black and white notes on the keyboard as F Major scale.

Improvisation suggestion.

Improvise a short piece in the Dorian Mode on G, using similar scalic runs to the piece on the facing page.

This piece is-based upon Unison figures at the distance of three octaves.

The changing time-signatures should flow from one to another quite smoothly.

The piece was inspired by the music of Jazz Pianist, Oscar Peterson, and is intended to convey the idea of 'possums scurrying about.

9. THE RING-TAIL 'POSSUM

RIVERSIDE SCENE

This piece is a chord and pedal study. Take the quarter note as the beat note using the bar lines as a guide to the strong beats.

Lydian Mode on C

Keep in mind that this Mode has the same pattern of black and white notes on the keyboard as G Major scale.

Chord analysis: Cmaj7 D7 Emj7 F#ø Gmaj7 Ami7 Bmi7 Cmaj7

Improvisation suggestion

Improvise a short chordal piece based on the Lydian Mode on C. Refer to the Chord analysis above.

10. RIVERSIDE SCENE

11. THE RARE NEW-HOLLAND MOUSE

This is a study in staccato and syncopation. Try to keep all the sixteenth-notes very light. Notice that the melody lies in the Bass part for the first six bars in each half.

12. THE WOMBAT

This is a Canon with variations. Note the changing registers and the different effects these create.

13. THE SQUIRREL GLIDER

This 7/8 piece is constructed of two different groupings:
a) 2-3-3 for example bars 2 and 3.
b) 3-2-2 example bars 4 and 5. Count the quavers (eighth-notes) very carefully.

THE SPINY ANT-EATER

This is another Serial composition, (refer to No. 6).
The repeated sections may be played as many times as the performer wishes.

THE ROW

Cluster notation — Play all the notes on the connected stems simultaneously.

14. THE SPINY ANT-EATER

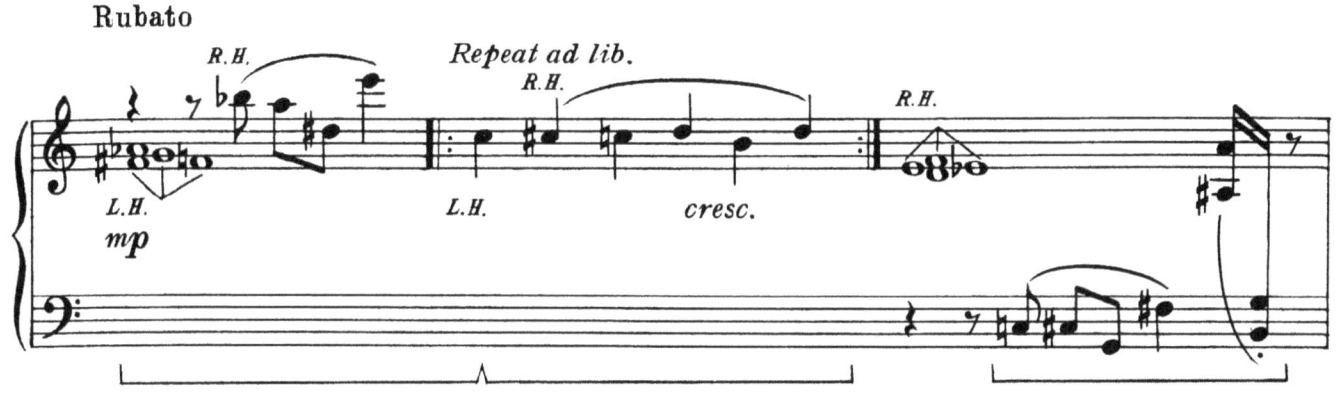

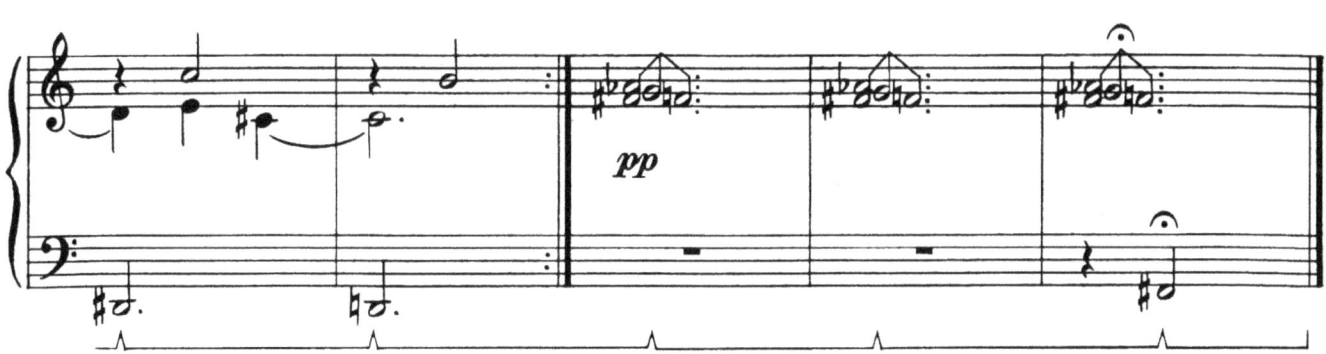

15. THE MOUNTAIN PYGMY POSSUM

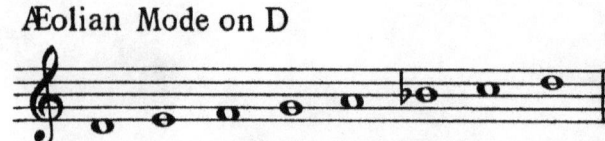

Remember that the pattern of black and white notes on the keyboard for this mode, is the same as for F Major scale.

Keep the broken chord figures very light and shimmery while bringing the left hand melody into the foreground.

Leggiero

THE SHORT-NOSED BANDICOOT

Mixolydian Mode on F

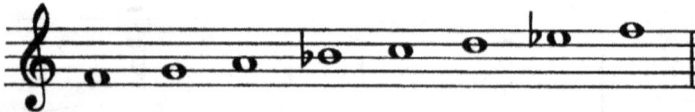

Remember that the pattern of black and white notes on the keyboard for this Mode is the same as for B flat Major scale.

Though this piece is in 5/4 time it is not grouped the same way throughout. Make the quarter-note (crotchet) the beat and place the smaller value notes accordingly.

The answering part in the Canon begins at the distance of five crotchet beats, but is brought closer to the distance of three beats at bar six. Note also the crossing of hands in bars six and nine.

Improvisation suggestion.

Improvise a short piece using the Mixolydian Mode on F, employing some of the devices, (Clusters, Rippling figures, etc.) so far discovered in this book.

16. THE SHORT NOSED BANDICOOT

17. THE GREY KANGAROO

This piece is a study in syncopation in triple time. Note the use of the Modal chords. The idea of 'bouncing kangaroos' can be brought out by the answering themes, and by the jagged effects of the syncopation.

Phrygian Mode on G

Remember that this mode has the same keyboard pattern of black and white notes as E flat Major scale.

Chord analysis

Improvisation suggestion.

Improvise a short piece on the given Mode using similar syncopated effects to those demonstrated in this piece.

Allegro non troppo

THE GREAT GLIDER-'POSSUM

As this piece is written without bar lines, take the quarter-note as the beat note and play each unit accordingly.

Try to achieve a smooth gliding sensation in your interpretation of this piece.

Phrygian Mode on C sharp

Remember that this Mode has the same keyboard pattern of black and white notes as A Major scale.

18. THE GREAT GLIDER-'POSSUM

19. THE RED KANGAROO

The accents in this piece of music in 7/8 time are placed on the sub-groups of 2-2-3. However, as the pattern is used over two bars and is tied across the bar line, it differs from the sound of the usual 2-2-3 grouping. Note also the use of thirds and fifths in the left hand part.

Lydian Mode on A

Remember that this Mode has the same keyboard pattern of black and white notes as E Major scale.

Pedal discreetly throughout

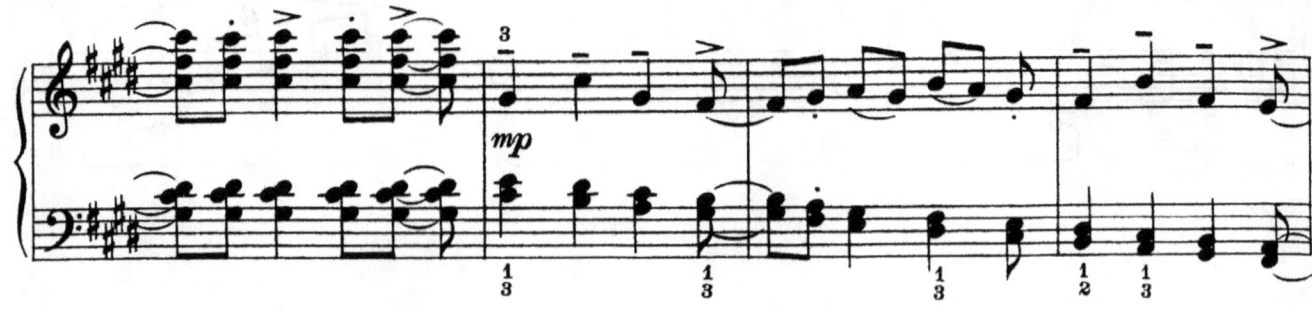

THE LOCRIAN MODE

Prior to the sixteenth century, the theory and practice of Modal music did not recognise this Mode as a separate scale. It was not until the Swiss theorist Henricus Glareanus, also known as 'Glarean (1488-1563), modified the old theory of Ecclesiastical Modes in his treatise *Dedocachordon (Twelve Modes or Twelve Keys)*, that the Mode was at the least recognised, although it was dismissed as being impracticable owing to the interval of a Diminished fifth between the Finalis (Tonic) and the Dominant.

By the 1570s, the Modes were reorganized so that the Ionian Mode (Major scale) was numbered as 1 and the other six followed in the sequence in which we know them to-day, although in practice the Locrian Mode was still not used, by the composers of Modal music.

However, since the beginning of the Twentieth Century the Mode has become a favourite of many jazz musicians, who overcome the problem of finality by altering the final chord to a Major or Minor chord. It is also very useful as a scale for improvising over the Half-diminished seventh chord (Minor seventh flattened fifth), in chord sequences such as -
I ii viiø I in a Major key.

Locrian Mode on B

Complete the seventh chords on the Mode and then name and play them.

e.g. Bø   Cmaj7   ....

The Emu

20. THE EMU

Improvisation suggestion

Improvise a short piece using the Locrian Mode on B over the B half-diminished seventh (B minor seventh flattened fifth chord).

THE PLATYPUS

Pentatonic Scale. Black notes only

Use the pedal discreetly to bring out the sonorities of the Pentatonic scale and to suggest the swimming motion of the Platypus in the river.

Improvisation suggestion

Improvise a free piece using the Pentatonic scale on the black notes only. Experiment with such techniques as playing clusters of notes with the flat of the hand, or with the clenched fist and playing *glissandi* on the black notes by sliding the flat of the hand along the keys.

21. THE PLATYPUS

MODERN CHORD SYMBOLS

Type of chord	Indicated by	Example
Major Triad	Letter name only	G
Minor Triad	mi or m	Gmi or Gm
Diminished Triad	Small circle after the letter	G°
Augmented Triad	Plus sign after the letter	G⁺
Suspended 4th Triad	Sus 4	Gsus4
Four-note chords		
Dominant 7th	7	G7
Major 7th	Maj7	Gmaj7
Minor 7th	mi7 or m7	Gmi7 or Gm7
Diminished 7th	Small circle and 7 after the letter or Dim7	G°7 Gdim7
Half-Diminished 7th	Small circle cut through	Cø or Cø7
Minor 7th Flattened 5th	mi7♭5	C7♭5
Major 6th	6	G6
Minor 6th	mi6	Gmi6

For further details on the construction and application of the above chords refer to:
* Contemporary Theory Workbooks 1 and 2
* Contemporary Chord Workbooks 1 and 2
* Contemporary Piano Method Books 1 through 4